Images of America
Lake Shore Cemetery of Avon Lake

This view of Avon Lake's historic, and only, cemetery reveals an eclectic array of tombstones. Worn by the elements and the ravages of time, these stones now reveal little of the stories of the deceased buried beneath each marker. Vintage newspapers, probate records, recollections shared by descendants, and local legends combine to reconstruct intriguing bits of history that tell the story of the evolution of a community. (Andrew Fowkes Photography.)

ON THE COVER: This view of Lake Shore Cemetery looking south shows the enduring charm of Avon Lake's shoreline burial ground. Photographer Andrew S. Fowkes is a direct descendant of the Tomanek family, many of whom are buried in the cemetery. His photographs fill out the various stories shared on the pages of this book. (Andrew Fowkes Photography.)

IMAGES
of America

LAKE SHORE CEMETERY OF AVON LAKE

Sherry Newman Spenzer
for Heritage Avon Lake

ARCADIA
PUBLISHING

Copyright © 2019 by Sherry Newman Spenzer for Heritage Avon Lake
ISBN 978-1-4671-0371-8

Published by Arcadia Publishing
Charleston, South Carolina

Library of Congress Control Number: 2019934375

For all general information, please contact Arcadia Publishing:
Telephone 843-853-2070
Fax 843-853-0044
E-mail sales@arcadiapublishing.com
For customer service and orders:
Toll-Free 1-888-313-2665

Visit us on the Internet at www.arcadiapublishing.com

To Charlotte Mallery Bowyer, bright hope of the future.

CONTENTS

Acknowledgments		6
Introduction		7
1.	First to Arrive, First to Depart	9
2.	The Grim Reaper, Dressed as Disease	21
3.	Names on Graves, Names on Streets	25
4.	Angel of Death and Innocent Babes	53
5.	From Germany to Erie's Shore	61
6.	There's No Place like Home	71
7.	Under One Roof but Different Directions	75
8.	Tales from beneath the Turf	87
9.	Lives Well Lived	113
10.	Tending the Cemetery	119

Acknowledgments

This book would not have been possible without the talent, patience, and commitment of photographer Andrew S. Fowkes, who tolerated repeated requests for "just one more photo" and provided beautiful work that ultimately became the backbone of this volume. To him, I owe the deepest debt of gratitude. Appreciation is also extended to Barb Cagley and Stephanie Biggers, who were of the greatest assistance in providing scans of vintage photographs, and to Jennifer Wasserman for her proofreading support. Special thanks also go to Tony Tomanek and his family, who were most generous in providing photographs and history relating to their many family members who are buried in Lake Shore Cemetery; Ronald and Marie Thomas, who provided family genealogical information; Megan Miller, who provided photographs from a private family collection; Sue Gerbick and Cindy McGuire, who shared family photographs and history; and Gerry Vogel and Avon Lake Public Library, for collecting and preserving numerous Avon Lake images. It has been my pleasure to work with Caroline Anderson, title manager at Arcadia Publishing, who has been most helpful throughout the publication process. Lastly, my deepest and most sincere respect is extended to those who populate Lake Shore Cemetery, as it was they who settled, built, and left the community of Avon Lake to the residents in whose charge the city now rests.

Original photographs in this volume are courtesy of Andrew Fowkes Photography (AFP).

Other images are courtesy of Avon Lake Public Library (ALPL) and Lorain County Probate Court (LCPC). Many of these images may also be found in the Cleveland Memory Project, Michael Schwartz Library at Cleveland State University, http://images.ulib.csuohio.edu/SpecColl (CMP). Public documents, including Ohio marriage certificates (OMC) and Ohio death certificates (ODC), are from "Ohio Deaths, 1908–1953," and "Ohio, County Marriages, 1789–2013," database with images, FamilySearch.org.

INTRODUCTION

Narrowly ensconced between a boat launch and an imposing fieldstone house beckons a small yet intriguing cemetery. Formally established when Avon Lake was still a part of Avon, Ohio, it is here that many of Avon Lake's first families, and members of their successive generations, occupy their final resting places. Only the deceased would find peace in this tract that commands no notice.

There are some who, although residents of the community, are unaware of this unobtrusive little cemetery's existence. Nevertheless, its stones stand sentry as solemn reminders of the hardships and challenges endured by those bold enough to first enter an untamed swampland and impose upon it the structure of farmlands, government, and culture. Names on tombstones are reflected on the city's streets, attracting the attention of those who are astute devotees of local history.

Bounded on the north by Lake Erie, whose sprays of ice and angry winter waves slap at the tiny graveyard during Ohio's inclement months, such ground seems a fit place for the burial of those whose lives were cut short by the rigors of farming, the perils of sailing, and the ravages of disease. Stone clumps are all that remain of some of the memorials that bear quiet witness to these lives long ago departed.

Known originally as Avon Lake Cemetery, and later as Lake Shore Cemetery, this burial spot offers no formal entrance—no vine-covered arch or stone pillars to welcome its visitors. Many of the gravestones are broken or completely illegible, eroded by time and neglect. Between some of the more solid and enduring markers are tiny mounds of peeling stone or aged shale. Every year tears away another of their layers, leaving a diminishing record of these silent residents.

Legend holds that the burial ground harbors the remains of French soldiers or traders and Native Americans who died on their journeys. While no graves of French soldiers or traders reveal themselves today, families from England, Ireland, Scotland, and Germany were neighbors in life and then in death in Avon Lake's only graveyard. Their infants became companions in eternity when their young lives were claimed by the scourge of typhoid, scarlet fever, influenza, and other poorly understood and unsuccessfully treated childhood diseases. Unmarked locations hold those who were stillborn or who survived no more than hours or days. Other rectangular-shaped sunken patches of earth suggest burials, but offer nothing more.

The temptation to romanticize the past can be seductive, but the lives of Avon Lake's dearly departed were not so very different from those of the people of its present. The stories of the "residents" of Avon Lake's cemetery offer a snapshot of an early community life in which its members met and married each other, cheated on and divorced each other, sheltered and sued each other, endured scandals and loss, did political battle, administered medical aid, and buried each other.

Some devoted themselves to sailing, others to farming, and still others to development of the community's government. Some were consumed by lives of sorrow, and some led lives of wantonness and folly. A man declared "lunatic" and another declared "drunkard" by a probate court in an era unaffected by political correctness is joined by a Ku Klux Klansman. All were part of the birth and growth of a community that overcame its darker history and remains and thrives today. Be it simple or remarkable, each of those buried in Lake Shore Cemetery's earth leaves a story. Some of the "inconvenient facts," far more comfortably heard when safely told in the past tense, still contain relevance and permit us access to a greater knowledge of the past.

A survey of the cemetery, conducted and compiled by the Genealogical Workshop of the Lorain County Historical Society of Elyria, Ohio, in 1980, identified approximately 150 burials by way of visible markers. Death certificates, family histories, and old newspaper articles accounting for unmarked burial sites expanded the number of interments to over 200. A rosebush, removed by city workers when its thorny branches became unruly and hostile, may once have been planted as a living memorial. Other graves, no longer marked by any remaining edifice, have been inadvertently discovered in more recent decades during the process of erecting flagpoles or digging for electrical installations. Another marker, found by city workers at the foot of the lake's cliff, was recovered and placed near its owner's spouse, as the precise location of its owner's plot was unknown.

A few graves gave just enough information to entice, but evaded accurate identification before they were lost. Such was the case with a stone that showed only a few discernible letters and appeared to indicate "Ranps." Another bore only the readable "J. Hore" and appeared also to have "CW" inscribed upon it. Both of those stones have disappeared, and whether "CW" designated yet another veteran of the Civil War has not been confirmed.

What appears to be a somewhat more contemporary marker also leaves its visitors with limited identifying information. "George Clark" does not share birth or death information or middle initial, and he is not buried near anyone who shares his last name. Rather than submitting to the temptation to speculate as to George Clark's identity, he receives mention here but is not included in the body of this work.

Today, the cemetery captures some measure of local interest each year when it becomes the site of Memorial Day observances. The solemn ground holds the remains of a Revolutionary War soldier, veterans of the War of 1812, several Civil War and World War I soldiers, and a World War II Army Air Corps serviceman. Roll call of the dead is conducted under the direction of American Legion Post 211 each year, as names of all deceased Avon Lake veterans who served their country are read aloud and publicly remembered.

The full measure of Lake Shore Cemetery's population will never be known, but every effort has been made to include in this volume as many of the names and stories of the cemetery's permanent residents as was possible.

One
FIRST TO ARRIVE, FIRST TO DEPART

Lake Shore Cemetery is a repository of Avon Lake's history, with its stories told on its stones. Some are generous with information, and others are stingy. Solitary stones mark unknown occupants, and monuments memorialize men and women who built a city. Even legend, kept alive through the generations, earned a permanent place in local history when two of Avon Lake's earliest burials were confirmed long after interment. (AFP.)

According to long-standing legend, the bodies of two sailors from the 1813 Battle of Put-In-Bay washed ashore near Avon Lake's cemetery and were buried by passersby. Theirs would have been the earliest known burials here. Though discounted by some of Avon Lake's early historians as an unlikely tale, the legend persisted, and a marker was placed in 2013 memorializing the unidentified seamen. (AFP.)

The legend was substantiated in 2015 when the seamen were identified by author-historian William Krejci (pictured) as Richard Williams and Henry VanPoole. During ship transport to Pennsylvania for treatment of their wounds, the pair died of typhus, and their bodies thrown overboard. A muster list of marines from Erie, Pennsylvania, and a letter to Naval Secretary Wiliam Jones dated September 22, 1813, confirm their identities. (Courtesy of Tom Krejci.)

The headstone of Edmunds Tower is the oldest standing legible stone in Lake Shore Cemetery. Though darkened by age and the elements, the marker remains decipherable. It reads: "Edmunds Tower of Ira, State of Vermont, was drowned the 9 June 1822, In the 22 year of his age." His first name, Edmunds, was his mother's maiden name. A first cousin once removed—Alexander Edmunds—is also buried in the cemetery. (AFP.)

The weathered stone of Sophia Woodruff shares substantial genealogy. It reads: "Sophia M., wife of Harvey Woodruff & dau. of Nathaniel Leete of W. Stockbridge, Mass. D. June 16, 1836 aged 25 yrs." The base is inscribed "Hail holy Angel sent to bring, The spirit of its promised rest, Raise your seraphic notes and sing, Th'eternal glories of the blessed." She left her husband a widower after just two years of marriage. (AFP.)

Near Sophia's grave is that of Zeruah M. Osgood, whose death followed just three months later. Zeruah came with her family to the lakeshore in 1827. She married Roland Osgood, the owner of a sawmill, when she was 18. Zeruah died September 11, 1836, at age 23. Her inscription reads, "The love that seems forsaken, When friend in death depart, In heaven again shall awken [sic], And repossess the Heart." (AFP.)

The headstone of Susan Case reveals little. She died January 15, 1850, at the age of 26. Her identity is confined to "wife of Isaac Case." In what is likely a result of the stonecutter's limited literacy, the s in Case is reversed, leaving a somewhat odd-looking memorial over her grave. Susan left a two-year-old son, and less than eight months after her death, Isaac took a second wife. (AFP.)

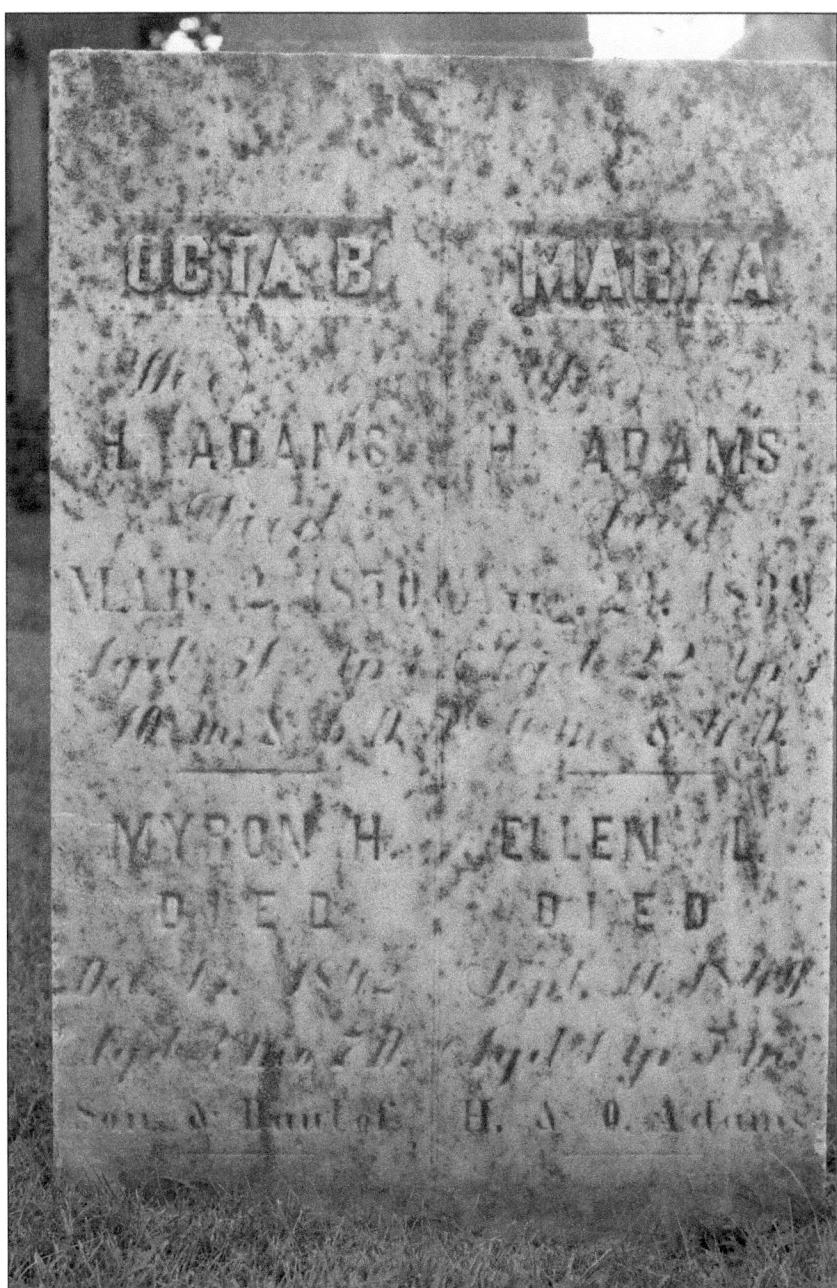

Among the older graves occupying the northwest section of Lake Shore Cemetery are those belonging to various members of the Adams family. The oldest of the Adams graves belongs to Mary, the first wife of William Harrison Adams. Mary died August 29, 1839, at the age of 22. Sharing her headstone is Octa Backus Strong, who was the second wife of William Harrison Adams. Married on March 9, 1841, Octa and William had three children, but only the last of these survived to adulthood. Their son Myron died in 1842 at the age of "3 months, 7 days," per the inscription on the communal headstone of the Adams wives. Daughter Ellen died September 11, 1849, at the age of one year and five months. Octa was pregnant with her third and last child at the time of Ellen's death. (AFP.)

Arthur Strong Adams was born to Octa and William on February 10, 1850. Octa survived Arthur's birth by only a few weeks and was laid to rest with her first two children—and William's first wife—on March 2, 1850. Arthur later became a physician and surgeon. Following years of ministering to the health of others, Arthur himself died of pneumonia and influenza on January 3, 1929. (AFP.)

Nettie Ford Adams, wife of Arthur, died August 20, 1924. The couple had no biological children. Nettie was buried in Lake Shore Cemetery near Arthur's mother. When Arthur died three and a half years later, he was buried near Nettie. Ironically, Arthur's death certificate lists his mother's name as "unknown," though she is buried less than five feet from him. (AFP.)

Estyes Matteson, the third of 13 children, was born in Vermont in 1791. In 1810, he married Lydia Phillips, and they migrated to Avon Lake after 1840. Limited sources suggest that Estyes saw battle in the War of 1812, a contention finding some support in his father's records. The elder Matteson joined the Chautauqua volunteers in defending Buffalo against British attack when Estyes was in his early 20s. Estyes may well have accompanied his father. (AFP.)

Lydia Matteson is buried with her husband. She married Estyes when she was 15 years old, and with him had seven children. Her husband died November 9, 1857, and she died a little more than five weeks later, on January 18, 1858. Two of their daughters married Jaycox men. Daughter Mary and her husband, George Jaycox, joined Estyes and Lydia in Lake Shore Cemetery, as did their 16-year-old son. (AFP.)

Among the cemetery's earlier marked burials are the final resting places of Lucy and Lyman Johnson, who left behind very limited details of their lives. Lyman died April 6, 1838, at the age of 61. He left his 47-year-old wife, Lucy, with a farm and 59 acres of land in Avon Lake. It appears that she was unsuccessful in the profitable management of the estate that was left to her. In 1843, the "heirs of Lyman Johnson" were listed on the county's delinquent land tax list. Lucy died December 14, 1844, at the age of 53. Though her upright standing stone has weathered well and is still entirely legible, her husband's marker is broken, with his death date concealed, and is now stacked as two pieces. Their burial sites are in the center of the cemetery. (AFP.)

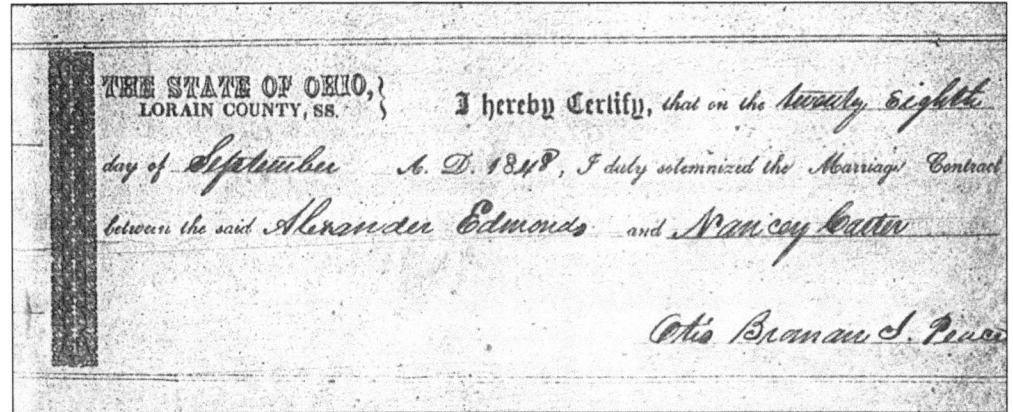

Alexander Edmunds of New York established himself as a successful farmer and owned 134 acres of land and considerable livestock in Avon Lake. He married Nancy Carter in 1848. Whatever his cause of death, he knew his demise was imminent. He dictated his last will and testament on June 17, 1856, and died July 1. He left Nancy a widow with two little sons, ages six and three. (OMC.)

The 1860 federal census lists the widowed Nancy Edmunds's occupation as "farmer." Shortly thereafter, she married John Patten, with whom she had a daughter, Elnora, in 1862. John died in 1872. Elnora died in 1891 and was buried with Alexander Edmunds. Nancy died in 1908, and joined her daughter and her first husband in Lake Shore Cemetery. (AFP.)

Among the early families to settle within Avon Lake was the Beard family. Phillip and Theressa Beard built a log cabin and raised five sons, Elmas being their eldest. Phillip left for the Civil War when Elmas was 14 and served until 1865. Theressa subsequently divorced Phillip, who lived with his sons until entering the Ohio Soldiers and Sailors Home in Sandusky, where he is buried. Elmas and his wife, Elizabeth, are buried in Lake Shore Cemetery. (AFP.)

Charles Beard (standing, far left) was one of Elmas Beard's younger brothers. Widowed in 1882, Charles was left with a son who was not yet two years old. In 1884, he married Malinda Titus, daughter of early Avon Lake settler Treat Titus, who came with his family to Avon Lake in 1829 and built a cabin near the lakeshore. (ALPL; Donor: Deb Beard.)

Malinda Titus Beard was one of 11 children. She was 27 years old when she married Charles. Aspiring to become a schoolteacher, she was a student at Oberlin College in Oberlin, Ohio. Her plans were aborted with the death of her mother in 1877, as Malinda was required to return home and keep house for her father and her older brothers. (Courtesy of Sue Gerbick.)

Charles Beard made his living as a fruit grower. Reputed to have had 1,000 fruit trees on his farm, he was particularly successful in growing grapes, which he sold to the Welch's company. He and Malinda had two daughters and a son. The generations that followed continue to gather and celebrate reunions in Avon Lake, and they are keenly devoted to the study and preservation of their genealogy. (Courtesy of Sue Gerbick.)

Charles Beard died in 1933 at the age of 80. Malinda survived him by 21 years, and she never remarried. She died in 1945 at the home of their eldest daughter in Bellevue, Ohio, where Malinda had relocated following her husband's death. Charles and Malinda are buried together in Lake Shore Cemetery. (AFP.)

Two

THE GRIM REAPER, DRESSED AS DISEASE

Allen Brown, aged "20y 6m 20d," lies beneath a stone that is now barely legible. A portion reads, "Although he is dead, He is speaking to you: Although he is dead, He invites you to come." Though appearing morbid, the memorial is more likely evangelism by Allen's Baptist minister father. The 1842 death was evidently a relief from suffering, as the epitaph concludes with "Sickness can never wreck His feeble frame again." (AFP.)

The headstone of Charles Ketchum flanks the eastern perimeter of the cemetery. Born in 1820, the Avon Lake farmer died December 1, 1852. A newspaper death notice reported that typhoid fever had claimed the man's life. There was no known prevention or cure for the disease at the time. Doctors attempted to treat typhoid patients with turpentine, quinine, and brandy, all without success. Ketchum became one of the unfortunate victims of the disease. (AFP.)

Albert Mitchell was born in 1826 in New York and married Charlotte Sheldon in 1848; they had two children. Albert had inherited extensive farmland acreage in Avon Lake where he and his family made their home. He died there December 28, 1852, at age 26, leaving a widow, a three-year-old daughter, and a one-year-old son. As his death occurred in the same month as that of neighbor Charles Ketchum, typhoid may offer an explanation for Albert's own premature demise. (AFP.)

Alexander Dunning Jr.'s grave is near those of Mitchell and Ketchum. Born in Ireland in 1833, the youth died November 19, 1852, at the age of "19y 9m," as inscribed on his headstone. As young Dunning's death preceded that of neighbor Charles Ketchum by less than two weeks, Alexander's death may also have been the result of typhoid, the trio of deaths suggesting an 1852 epidemic along the shore. (AFP.)

Victor Monroe Matteson, son of Estyes and Lydia Matteson, died August 22, 1850. He lived "sixteen years, five months, and nine days" according to his headstone, which bears the touching inscription: "Being himself amiable and lovely was loved by all." The cause of death is not identified. He is buried near his parents, his sister Mary Jaycox, and his nephew Charles Jaycox. (AFP.)

This tortured soul, whose name appears only as "H. Trask" on his headstone, left little from which to understand his life. A local paper carried nothing more than "Suicide. A citizen of Avon, named Trask, hung himself last week." Trask died on December 18, 1849, leaving a 48-year-old widow, Mary, to survive him. His stone is no longer legible, and the cause of his torment, be it physical or other, will likely remain forever unknown. (AFP.)

Three

NAMES ON GRAVES, NAMES ON STREETS

Samuel and Sarah Jacox of New York settled near Erie's shore with their family in 1828. Some sources suggest that Samuel also served in the War of 1812. The couple's tombstone tells the story of their January 1855 demise: "death caused by suffocation by a kettle of coals in their sleeping room." Subsequent generations adopted the variant "Jaycox" spelling. The name endures as one of Avon Lake's main north-south streets. (AFP.)

The gravestone of Laura, daughter of Samuel and Sarah Jacox, has frequently been misidentified as the gravesite of her husband. The stone, originally inscribed "Laura, Wife of Charles Mitchell," is broken off above Charles's name. The broken remnant has thus suggested to visitors that it is the grave of Charles, and not that of Laura Mitchell Jacox, misleading genealogists and causing confusion in the research of some. The unsecured broken piece has been moved to various locations in the cemetery, and at present is propped against the cemetery shelter. The true site of Laura's burial within the grounds is no longer known. She died in 1847 at the age of "44y 5m 18d," per the original inscription. Investigation by some genealogists indicates that a daughter was born to Laura in 1847. If accurate, Laura's death may have occurred as a consequence of childbirth. (AFP.)

Samuel and Sarah Jacox's son, George Jaycox, is buried near them. The spelling of the family's last named changed with his generation. A prominent citizen of the community, Jaycox held various township offices, was a successful farmer, and owned substantial acreage. Generous and community-minded, he donated land for one of the village's first schoolhouses. He married Mary Matteson in 1841, and the couple had 10 children. (AFP.)

In the year prior to his 1874 death, George Jaycox completed construction of his family's new home. Upon his demise, he left four minors, four adult children, a son-in-law, and his wife to occupy the dwelling. The home is still standing, its vintage beauty carefully preserved by its present occupant-owners, who continue to maintain the structure as a single-family residence. (Photograph by author.)

This memorial to Capt. John Duff marks his memory, but not his remains. A 30-year sailing veteran and skilled shipbuilder, he was hailed as a master of the lakes. Despite his maritime skills, his life was cut short when his ship, the *C.B. Benson*, capsized in a violent Lake Erie storm on October 14, 1893. The captain's wife, Caroline Curtis Duff, died 21 years later and is buried at this site. (AFP.)

With the sinking of the *C.B. Benson*, all hands were lost, including Curtis Duff, the captain's son. Curtis's wife frequently accompanied the crew as ship's cook. Initially reported by newspapers as one of the vessel's casualties, she was pregnant when the ship made its inauspicious voyage and elected to forego the journey. Though her life was spared, her son was rendered fatherless immediately upon his birth. (ALPL; Donor: Gerry Paine.)

Curtis Duff's son was born April 29, 1894, more than six months after the infant's father perished on the ill-fated *C.B. Benson*. The widow named her son (pictured here) Curtis Duff, after his father. Although born in Port Clinton, Ohio, the child was brought by his mother back to Avon Lake, where extended family helped to raise him. (ALPL; Donor: Gerry Paine.)

John Duff, Captain Duff's eldest son, began his career as a sailor and later became a skilled shipbuilder, often sailing with his father and brother. When his fiancée's mother opposed her daughter's marriage to a sailor, John left sailing to pursue a career in law. This fortuitous career change spared him the fate of his father and brother. (Courtesy of Dawn Austin.)

John Duff distinguished himself as a respected jurist and served an unexpired term as a common pleas judge in Ottawa County. Although he abandoned sailing as a profession, he was remembered as a man of remarkable physical strength who always owned a pleasure craft of some type. Upon his untimely death at the age of 65, his family had his remains buried in Avon Lake's cemetery near his mother. (AFP.)

Captain Duff's daughter Nellie A. Duff is buried next to her brother John. In 1885, Captain Duff's schooner *Nellie A. Duff* was built in Port Clinton, Ohio. In an uncanny twist of fate, the *Nellie A. Duff* sank in Lake Erie with a loss of three of its four crew members. The date of the disaster was October 14, 1895—exactly two years after the sinking of the *C.B. Benson*. (AFP.)

Alta Duff Bliss is interred in the plot next to her sister Nellie. She married Clark W. Bliss in 1902, and in 1904, their daughter Caroline was born. Alta was widowed in 1910 after her husband contracted tuberculosis. He spent his final months at his family home in Pennsylvania, where he is interred. Alta was buried with her mother and siblings in Avon Lake upon her death in 1961. (AFP.)

Buried next to her mother is Caroline Alta Bliss. She was just six years old when her father died. She showed an early aptitude for art, winning awards for her various projects, and later attended the Cleveland School of Art. She never married, but remained active in artistic and musical endeavors. Upon her death in 1985, the profession listed on her death certificate was "painter, sculptor, craft-artist, and artist printmaker." (AFP.)

William Joel Curtis, brother of Caroline Curtis Duff, was a longtime lake boat captain and is fittingly interred along the lake's shore with his several family members. His wife, Mary Jane (Cuyler) Curtis, was his first cousin, a union sanctioned by Ohio law at the time the couple married in 1889. (AFP.)

As captain of the schooner *General Franz Seigel*, William Joel Curtis also met fickle Lake Erie's wrath. In July 1903, he, his wife, and a crew of three more were caught in a storm while hauling coal. The ship sank in 22 feet of water. All five climbed the rigging in retreat from peril, where they awaited rescue. Their lives were saved, but the ship was a total loss. (AFP.)

In the next census following the loss of his 40-year-old ship, *General Franz Seigel*, Captain William Joel Curtis no longer listed his occupation as "sailor" as he had in previous censuses. Instead, he identified himself as a farmer, working on his "own account" in Avon Lake. (ALPL; Donor: Gerry Paine.)

Captain Curtis's wife, Mary Jane (back row far right), waited three hours before being rescued from the *Franz Seigel*. The harrowing experience was a testament to the tough woman's mettle. She and her husband later raised Curtis Paul Duff, as his mother died when the boy was just 13 years old. Having no children of her own, Mary Jane left her estate to Curtis when she died in 1931. (ALPL; Donor: Gerry Paine.)

Just before his 24th birthday, Curtis Paul Duff enlisted in the military. He served in World War I from July 1918 to June 1919, achieving the rank of sergeant in May 1919. He was one of Avon Lake's early councilmen and a director of the Ohio Fruit Growers Co-operative Association. He shares a headstone with his wife, Dorothy Mitchell Duff; both died in 1982. (AFP.)

Curtis and Dorothy Duff, who had two children, are joined by a granddaughter, Sally Filker Carney, who is buried near them in Lake Shore Cemetery. Born in 1948 in Avon Lake, Sally was only 38 years old at the time of her death in 1986 after a short illness. (AFP.)

This home on the shore in Avon Lake was the residence of several generations of Curtis and Duff families, and it remains standing today. In its front yard is one of the anchors from the *C.B. Benson*, the schooner that claimed the lives of Captain Duff and his son. Avon Lake streets bear the names of Duff and Curtis, leaving another lasting reminder of the seafaring family. (ALPL; Donor: Gerry Paine.)

Lake Shore Cemetery's earliest veteran is Joseph Moore, who died February 19, 1846. Distinguished by his Revolutionary War service, Moore enlisted in the Massachusetts Continental army in 1780, and served until the conclusion of the war in 1783. Multiple sources identify him as one of Gen. George Washington's bodyguards. He identifies himself as a Revolutionary War veteran in his last will. The now illegible inscription on his headstone, transcribed verbatim, is "Imigrant from New England, defiran the revolution of 76." (AFP.)

Buried next to Joseph Moore is his wife, Hannah. A tree trunk had enveloped her tombstone, leaving the reconstructed marker incomplete after the tree's removal. Hannah bore Joseph 11 children, and by her 57th birthday was described as "very feeble and almost blind." She died in 1842. The couple was allegedly survived by over 80 grandchildren, and Avon Lake's Moore Road is named for Steve Moore, one of their many grandsons. (AFP.)

North of Hannah Moore's grave is that of her son Ransom Moore. Now nearly illegible, his stone is etched with a weeping willow. A lake boat captain by occupation, Ransom was born in 1805 and died in August 1837. The assets listed in his estate included a colt, four hogs, three cows, barrels, kettles, chests, a clock, 18 pounds of tallow, a wagon, and—indicative of the perils faced by early Avon Lake settlers—a bear trap. (AFP.)

Fred Beck and his brother Henry were sons of immigrant German farmers Lawrence and Amelia Beck, who moved to Avon Lake in the early 1870s. Henry was born in 1876, and Fred was born in 1881. The brothers worked the family farm as young men, later purchasing additional acreage in Avon Lake, which they divided and farmed as their own. Here, a dapper-looking Fred stands with his horse amidst his chickens. (ALPL; Donor: Paul Beck.)

In 1907, Fred Beck married Wilhelmina "Minnie" Paschen, daughter of German-born parents, whose last name sometimes appeared as "Parschen." Fred was 25 when they married, and Minnie was 18. They had one son. In this later photograph on their farm, Minnie appears at far right, with their son Walter at far left. (ALPL; Donor: Paul Beck.)

Fred Beck died February 6, 1935, at age 53, survived by his wife and son. Minnie remarried several years later. Both Fred and Minnie are buried in Avon Lake's cemetery, along with Minnie's second husband, Thomas Kenny, who worked as a foreman at the Standard Sewing Machine Company in Cleveland. Minnie died in 1971, although no year of death appears on her headstone. (AFP.)

Fred's older brother Henry Beck married Emma Herrmann in 1899. Henry died October 6, 1929, just eight weeks before his son Emil, who is laid to rest near his father. The Beck farmland was later subdivided for residential development, but the Beck family left its name, as Beck Road remains to identify the general location of their former farmland. (AFP.)

Henry and Emma's son Emil lost his life in a tragic vehicular accident on November 26, 1929. The handsome and single young man was just two months shy of his 25th birthday when he died. He was attempting to light a cigarette while driving and collided with a truck, which turned over twice and caught fire. The truck driver survived, as did Beck's passenger. Beck did not. (AFP.)

Emma's family, the Herrmanns, established a restaurant and tourist inn business in Avon Lake. After Henry's death and many years of widowhood, Emma married her daughter-in-law's father, Peter Ebach, a widower. Upon Emma's death, her remains were brought to lie at the side of Henry and their son Emil in Lake Shore Cemetery. (AFP.)

Eugene Herrmann Sr. was born in Germany in 1854 and immigrated to the United States when he was 18. He was married in 1877, and with his wife, Caroline, settled along the shore in Avon Lake, where they established a fruit farm. The couple had three children—Emma (Mrs. Henry Beck), Fred, and Eugene Jr. Caroline died in 1838, surviving her husband by three and a half years. (AFP.)

Eugene Herrmann Jr. married Myrtle Martin in 1915. Both enjoyed an active social life. Myrtle embraced the flapper era and was known to dress the part. Eugene played drums in a local band and frequently appeared at Avon Lake's legendary Lake Shore Inn, a favorite roadhouse during Prohibition that was lost to an unsolved act of arson in 1926. (Courtesy of Megan Miller.)

Eugene Jr. (pictured) and Myrtle operated a roadside stand, seen here, and later opened the Herrmann-Martin Tourist Inn in a farmhouse that was moved from its original site. A restaurant was in the front of the house, and Eugene Jr. built several cottages on adjoining property. The cottages were offered for rent and drew tourists eager to enjoy summer weather tempered by Lake Erie breezes. (Courtesy of Megan Miller.)

Both locals and tourists frequented the Herrmann-Martin establishment. The couple and their daughter lived upstairs at the inn until Eugene Jr. completed construction of their family home across the street. The restaurant occasionally hosted a young Guy Lombardo for meals in the performer's early days when he traveled the roadhouse circuit. (Courtesy of Megan Miller.)

The Herrmanns actively ran their business for 17 years. In the mid-1950s, they leased the operation to a local who opened Stephen's Market. The tourist cottages were eventually torn down, but the establishment remained. It changed hands several times during its lifetime, but continued as a restaurant or lounge under the control of various owners. (ALPL; Donor: John Earley.)

Never idle, Eugene Jr. later worked as a night clerk at the famed Saddle Inn (pictured), an Avon Lake restaurant and hotel that was frequented by celebrities and politicians. He also worked as a clerk in the local liquor store. He died in 1981, and with his wife, is buried near his parents and his sister Emma Herrmann Beck. (ALPL; Donor: Fred Bottomer.)

Myrtle died in 1986 at the age of 90. She had been a resident of Avon Lake for 80 years. Aside from the business that she actively comanaged with her husband and for which she worked as a cook, the civic-minded woman was also a cofounder of Avon Lake's municipal park. (AFP.)

Remarkably, the business that Eugene Jr. and Myrtle began more than a century ago remains standing and continues to function as a popular eatery. It now operates as Jake's on the Lake, and the original architecture remains nearly unchanged. Hanging on the walls are charming photographs that chronicle the history of the establishment since its first ownership by the Herrmanns, and west of the business is Herrmann Drive, memorializing the family name. (Photograph by author.)

Anton H. Tomanek immigrated from Moravia with his family in 1865 on the ship *Leocadia*. The family settled first in Cleveland, then relocated to Avon Lake where they cultivated vineyards, fruit trees, grapes, and a variety of berries, all of which proliferated in the soil south of Lake Erie. Upon his father's death, Anton inherited a farm of roughly 33 acres. (AFP.)

In 1886, Anton married Clara Frey. Born in a log cabin in Avon Lake, she lived all 93 years of her life in that city. Her eldest child, Mayme, was adopted, and her union with Anton produced four sons and a daughter. She served the community as a midwife and bade three of her sons farewell when they served in World War I. All three returned. (Courtesy of the Tomanek family.)

Anton Tomanek was appointed the town's postmaster in 1893 and started the first residential delivery system, taking mail to peoples' homes once every week. His post office burned to the ground in 1899, though he succeeded in saving most of the mail. Several years later, the barn on his property caught fire. In 1912, lightning struck a third time, destroying the family's home. In his later years, Anton earned the nickname of "Fifty-center" when, from his front porch, he would invite passersby to share in a little of his homemade wine, and would gift them with 50¢. He died at the age of 64. The street transecting the family's farm was to be named Tomanek, but due to an error in transcription, was instead designated "Tomahawk," which it remains today. (Courtesy of the Tomanek family.)

While the Tomanek brothers (first, third, and fourth from left) enjoyed staging a humorous scene, all had a serious side as well. Three served their country in the armed forces, one served several terms as village marshal, another as a deputy marshal and volunteer fireman, and all maintained roots in their community. (Courtesy of the Tomanek family.)

Anton and Clara Tomanek's eldest son, Robert, enlisted in the US Marine Corps in Cleveland in June 1918, just two years after he was married. Upon completion of his service in World War I, he was granted an honorable discharge on April 29, 1919, in Philadelphia. (Courtesy of the Tomanek family.)

Following his discharge, Robert Tomanek returned to his carpentry work in Avon Lake and to his wife, Valborg. The couple had three daughters. Robert suffered a stroke in January 1938 when he was just 51. Although he survived, he lived only another six years. A cerebral hemorrhage claimed his life at the age of 57, and he died on May 2, 1945. His headstone reflects his military service. (AFP.)

Valborg Aslaksen Tomanek occupies a burial plot adjacent to her husband. She was the elder sister of Elizabeth Aslaksen; both sisters married Tomanek brothers. The daughter of renowned sea captain Olaf Aslaksen, who accompanied Roald Amundsen as second mate on the Belgian expedition to the Antarctic, Valborg was born in Port Stanley, Falkland Islands, in 1895 and was the oldest of the 13 Aslaksen children. (Courtesy of the Tomanek family.)

Valborg and Robert had four daughters. After her husband's death, she remained in Avon Lake, and in 1960, she took employment as a cook in the Avon Lake school system, from which she eventually retired. She never remarried and far outlived her husband, dying in 1993 at the age of 97. (AFP.)

Clara and Anton's second child, Frank, was their only son not to serve in the military. He was also the first child they buried. Married with a young son and awaiting his second child, Frank suffered a cerebral hemorrhage at the age of 30 when attempting to push a stalled car out of a ditch. Four weeks later, his second son was born to his widow. Clara, Anton, and Frank share a single headstone. (AFP.)

The third Tomanek son, William, married Elizabeth Aslaksen when he was 28 and she was 21. He was a carpenter like his brother Robert, and the Tomaneks built homes in Avon Lake, where they were lifelong residents. William and Elizabeth had four sons and three daughters. One of their sons, Richard, was a pitcher for the Cleveland Indians from 1957 to 1958, then was traded to the Kansas City Athletics. (Courtesy of the Tomanek family.)

William Tomanek served with the US Army in World War I. He was in the 112th Engineers (Cleveland Greys) and fought in the Meuse-Argonne Campaign, for which his company was awarded the French Croix de Guerre. Upon his return, he resumed his contractor work in Avon Lake, while also serving his community as a deputy marshal and a volunteer fireman. (AFP.)

William's wife is buried near him. Born Elizabeth Aslaksen, she was a younger sister of Valborg and a daughter of Capt. Olaf Aslaksen. Her mother was the child of British immigrants to the Falkland Islands. Elizabeth's own birthplace was Picton Island, Chile. The Aslaksen family moved to Cleveland in 1904, and eventually settled in Avon Lake, where Elizabeth and William were married in July 1920. (AFP.)

Clara and Anton's youngest son, Carl, served his country and then his community in multiple capacities. Like his older brother William, he joined the US Army's 112th Engineers in World War I. He was 19 years old and single when he enlisted, just one month after his brother William's enlistment. Carl was awarded a Bronze Victory Button for honorable service in active duty. (Courtesy of National Archives, archives.gov.)

Carl Tomanek became marshal of Avon Lake Village in 1925, earning a reputation for his aggressive pursuit of rumrunners during the Prohibition era. In 1928, he made headlines when he confiscated 27 cases of liquor that had been unloaded on a beach in Avon Lake after he and his deputy interrupted the illegal transaction. The transgressors fled to their boat and disappeared, and the contraband became property of law enforcement. In August 1929, Tomanek made another bust when he intercepted 19 cases of Canadian whiskey, which had been unloaded behind Avon Lake's illuminating plant, and took two rumrunners into custody. The haul was hailed as one of the county's largest of the year. Tomanek later became the first Avon Lake motorcycle policeman and a village fire marshal. In 1933, he was named "Grand Marshal of the Day" for the Memorial Day march to Avon Lake's cemetery—the future site of his own burial. (AFP.)

In 1941, Carl Tomanek was employed by the American Shipbuilding Company in Lorain, Ohio. He was exposed to a poisonous gas when fumes emanated from a cement used in construction of navy submarine net tenders on which he was working, resulting in his premature death at age 42. There was initial reluctance on the part of his employer to acknowledge the cause of death, but an investigation resulted in a finding of "inhaled toxin at work" on his death certificate. He was survived by a widow, a son, and a daughter. Although none are interred with him in Avon Lake's cemetery, he was joined by an infant son who died in 1928 three days after birth and has no marker. (ODC.)

Four

Angel of Death and Innocent Babes

Next to their father, Ransom Moore, lie the remains of children Helen and Jerome. Helen died in March 1836 at age 10. Jerome died in August 1837—the same month and year as his father. The child was one year and four months of age. While the cause of death is unknown for these children, Ransom's estate includes a receipt for a quart of French brandy provided to him "in his last sickness." Brandy was often administered to sufferers of typhoid. (AFP.)

Charles Rolfe leaves only oral history to explain his death and a weathered, barely legible stone to record his existence. Legend holds that 15-year-old Charles drowned when his family was here from Wisconsin to visit relatives. His epitaph once read "In memory of Charles W. Rolfe who died Oct. 7, 1839. Aged 15 years." The remnants of his stone are in two broken pieces, and the inscription is now nearly obscured. (AFP.)

Beneath a stone showing the wear of age and failed repairs lies 27-year-old Susan (née Farr), wife of Samuel C.P. Gillette. With her are daughter Lydia, who died in 1842 at the age of nine months, and 12-day-old infant Naomi, who died June 23, 1845. Susan died only nine days after her daughter Naomi, most likely from complications of childbirth. (AFP.)

After Susan Gillette's death, Samuel married Susan's sister, Abigail. Their son, S. Colon, died June 4, 1853, when he was only eight months and eight days old. Whatever affliction befell their son likely claimed their daughter, whom they also named Lydia. The little girl died three months after her brother, on September 2, 1853, when just five years, four months, and 19 days old. Both are buried with their aunt Susan and her two children. (AFP.)

Charles Jaycox, firstborn of George and Mary Jaycox, is buried with his parents in Lake Shore Cemetery. Charles died in 1852 of "scarlatina"—or scarlet fever—at the age of seven. His epitaph reads: "O ye mourners, cease to languish, o'er the grave of him you loved, far removed from pain and anguish, he's a-chanting hymns above." (AFP.)

Catherine "Kittie" Ketchum is buried with her grandparents Charles and Catherine Ketchum. The child died December 29, 1883, with no indication of cause of death. Her age at the time of her passing, as inscribed on her epitaph, was "13y, 4m, 17d." Her stone is remarkable despite its age, and has endured the harsh elements of the lakeshore. (AFP.)

Rose May Dunning, daughter of John and Mahala Dunning, died December 31, 1883, when she was "7y, 3m, 19d," according to the child's headstone. The cause of death attributed to her was simply "fits," a description that more aptly describes symptoms than a specific disease in an era when infectious diseases were poorly understood and doctors often had little to offer their ailing patients. (AFP.)

Four of Orlando and Eliza Jaycox Moore's five children died between 1882 and 1889. Of the four, none lived more than two years. The first loss was daughter Winnie, who lived only a year and was buried in 1882. The medical community being relatively helpless in combating childhood diseases, the deaths of three younger siblings followed in rapid succession. (AFP.)

Two-year-old Maud "Maudie" Moore, Orlando and Eliza's second child, died in 1885 of measles. Her short obituary in the now defunct *Elyria Republican* describes her as exhibiting "wonderful patience for one so young," and reads: "Just at the age of life so rich with love, her little life is hushed. Bright jewel; she is gone to sleep that dreamless sleep that kisses down the eyelids still." (AFP.)

The couple's next two infants, Earl and Almyra, died in 1887 and 1889. No cause of death is given for Earl, but Almira's demise was attributed to "brain fever," which was frequently used to describe the disease encephalitis. Almyra was born in the same year that her brother Earl died. (AFP.)

In 1926, scarlet fever claimed the life of another Avon Lake child. Herbert Wendt, a 13-year-old student, succumbed to the disease after just three days under a doctor's care. Ten months later, his brother Bernhardt died of peritonitis following a ruptured appendix. The brothers are buried together and share a common stone. (AFP.)

Buried in Lake Shore Cemetery in an unmarked grave is 16-year-old Elmer Krakow, a victim of the influenza epidemic of 1927–1928. Although not as calamitous as the influenza pandemic of 1918, the later wave of that fear-invoking disease again claimed a substantial number of lives. Both the young and the old were casualties. Elmer had endured a previous battle with pneumonia in 1915, and was reported by a local newspaper to have been "dangerously ill." Although he survived the illness on the first occasion, the youth lost his life on April 11, 1928, to pneumonia as a complication of influenza. His death certificate indicates that he was buried in Avon Lake's cemetery, and his occupation was listed as "scholar." Although his grandparents' burial plots are marked, neither he, his father, nor his mother have a headstone to mark their final resting place. (ODC.)

The latest burial of a child in Lake Shore Cemetery is that of two-year-old Dennis Ray Jockisch. Born in 1957, the child had been ill from the time of his birth, with frequent hospital stays. He died February 21, 1959. His headstone, with the inscription "Little Dennie," bears the carved image of a little curly-haired praying cherub. (AFP.)

Five

FROM GERMANY TO ERIE'S SHORE

Born to German immigrant parents in Avon Lake in 1860, Joseph Frye was the elder brother of Clara, wife of Anton Tomanek. In 1892, Joseph married Clotilda Spaetzel, with whom he had six children. They moved from their Avon Lake farm to Elyria, Ohio, around 1920. In March 1936, Joseph sustained serious trauma when he fell while driving a team of horses on his farm. He never recovered and died June 17, 1936. (AFP.)

Jacob Goepp was 20 years old when he immigrated from Germany. He became a naturalized citizen in 1858, worked as a machinist, and later operated a wallpaper store in Cleveland. He was registered for the draft in Ohio's 18th district during the Civil War, but sidestepped service by paying $550 to the district administrator to engage another draftee to serve in his place. (AFP.)

Jacob married Charlotte Roof in 1856. A native Clevelander, she worked first as a milliner, then later joined her husband in their wallpaper business, where she worked for 40 years before her death. The couple had four daughters, three of whom are buried with them in Lake Shore Cemetery, along with one granddaughter and one great-granddaughter. (AFP.)

Ferdinand Kotz, another German immigrant, married Lena Fritz in 1888, and together the couple worked a farm in Avon Lake. They had two sons and a daughter. In 1892, he became a naturalized US citizen, swearing an oath of loyalty to the Constitution and renouncing any allegiance to any other sovereignty, particularly "to William Emperor of Germany." (Courtesy of Bonita Hemminger Walker.)

The graves of Ferdinand and Lena are marked with tasteful headstones that have survived the elements. Both husband and wife died in 1924 and were mercifully spared the sorrow that followed. Their daughter, Lillian Kotz Krakow, died three years later in October 1927 of stomach and liver cancer. Their grandson, Elmer Krakow, died not long thereafter in April 1928 at the age of 16. (AFP.)

Lillian's husband, Louis Krakow, did not withstand the torment of such heavy loss. He committed suicide on July 11, 1930, by a gunshot to the head. Following the death of his wife, the death of his son, a failed second marriage, and $500 dollars in funeral debt, Louis left a signed note that said nothing more than "good bye." He, Lillian, and Elmer are all buried in unmarked graves in Lake Shore Cemetery. (AFP.)

Louis Krakow's parents, John and Sophia Bambam Krakow, predeceased him and are buried in marked graves. Born in Mecklenberg, Germany, the couple was married there in 1865. They were the parents of two sons and two daughters. Their first child was born in Germany, and the rest were born in Avon Lake. Sons Louis and Charles are buried in Lake Shore Cemetery with their parents, as are granddaughter Minnie (Parschen) Beck Kenny and Minnie's father, William Parschen. (AFP.)

Charles Krakow, a resident of Avon Lake for 81 years, died in 1968 and is at rest near his parents' burial sites. Divorced in 1914 from his first wife, with whom he had four children, Charles remarried and made a successful living as a contractor and builder, advertising his specialty to be "cottage and repair work." (ALPL; Donor: Barney Klement.)

Charles appears to have lived a socially active life in Avon Lake, as his name frequently appeared in local papers for receiving guests, "paying calls" to others, and hosting dances at his home. Unfortunately, he was also the victim of a theft in 1907 by one of the incorrigible sons of neighbor Daniel Green, the latter being buried not far from Charles. (Courtesy of J. Thompson.)

William Parschen was 44 years old when he succumbed to tuberculosis in 1909. He left a widow and three children, two of whom were minors. His eldest, Minnie, was married to Fred Beck. During William's lifetime, variant spellings of his German last name included Parschen, Parshen, Parshins, and Parchen. While "Parschen" appears on William's marriage and death certificates and as daughter Minnie's last name, it is "Paschen" that is etched upon his headstone. (AFP.)

Marked by a single stone bearing the Stein name lie brothers Frederick and Roswell Stein and their parents, Gustave and Lillian. Frederick died in 1926, and Roswell in 1929. Gustave owned substantial real estate in Avon Lake, but fell victim to the Depression, and in January 1936, the bank holding a mortgage on his property filed for foreclosure. Gustave died in February 1938. His wife, Lillian, died in December 1939. (AFP.)

John Schaefer was born in Germany in 1854, and between 1875 and 1880, lost his father, two brothers, and his mother. He left his homeland in 1882 and sailed to America, as did Fredericka Weik, whom he married in 1883 in Manistee, Michigan. They moved first to Cleveland, and then to Avon Lake, where John died in 1927 when stricken by influenza. (Courtesy of Margaret Ramsdell.)

John Schaefer's occupation appeared for years in census reports as "night watchman." At the time of his death, however, he was working as a wood finisher for Cleveland Window & Glass company. This is a view of the plant from the Main Avenue Bridge in Cleveland looking toward Lake Erie. (Courtesy of Cleveland Public Library Photograph Collection.)

Fredericka sailed to America from Germany in 1882 when she was just 19 years old. She married John Schaefer the following year, and the couple had three sons and a daughter. In the early 1920s, they lived in Avon Lake near Stop 46 of the Lake Shore Electric Railway. Fredericka died in Pittsburgh at the home of her daughter in 1939, but was brought back to Lake Shore Cemetery for burial with her husband. (AFP.)

Leonard Haag and Anna Scheible were married in 1906, and joined with Anna's German immigrant father in maintaining his farm, vineyards, and wine press operations along the lakeshore. Leonard also served the community as councilman commencing in the early 1920s, and was later village appraiser. They had two sons. Their younger son, Carl, was one of the village's first fire chiefs. (ALPL; Donor: Barney Klement.)

Anna's uncle Simon Scheible lived with her and Leonard on the family farm for many of his final years until his death in 1953. He is buried with the Haags and their grandsons, twins Thomas and Todd. The babies died in early infancy in July 1968, just months before their grandmother Anna's death in October 1968. All five share a common headstone. (AFP.)

Following the death of his German immigrant father, William R. Hinz, with his wife, his mother, and his mother's maidservant of 50 years, occupied the family homestead within Avon Lake's eastern limits. In 1926, a local paper included an article about eagles that had nested behind the Hinz home along the cliff above the lake. William and his wife lived the remainder of their lives in the family home. (Courtesy of Bay Village Historical Society.)

69

William was one of Avon Lake's first village officials, serving consecutive terms as clerk. He also served on the board of education in the early 1920s. With a vision for city development, he sought actively to entice the Ford Motor Company to build a plant in Avon Lake in 1930, but was rejected. In 1972, his wife, Ruth, died. In 1974, the year of William's death, Ford built a 419-acre plant in Avon Lake. (AFP.)

Six
There's No Place like Home

In 1868, Lorain County opened its poorhouse. The facility held paupers, elderly without family, and those adjudicated insane. Many of its "inmates" spent their final days there. Any inmate not claimed at death by a family member for burial was interred in an adjoining potter's field. Several of Avon Lake's dead expired in the poorhouse, but their remains were claimed by friends or family for burial in their hometown. (Courtesy Lorain County Historical Society.)

Civil War veteran Reed Manning died a widower in 1928 in the Lorain County Infirmary. Although it appears he was without funds or family, someone arranged for the man's body to be returned to his hometown for burial in Avon Lake's cemetery. His death certificate reveals that he was a veteran, but it offers no other genealogical information. (AFP.)

Wolcott Payne, another former poorhouse resident, is buried in Lake Shore Cemetery in an unmarked grave. Plagued by financial difficulties, he suffered a stroke in 1937, then lived briefly with his brother Carl. His draft registration reveals that by 1942, he was in the County Home, as the poorhouse was later named. He died there in 1956, leaving behind a trail littered with unpaid notes and debts to various residents of the Avon Lake community. (Courtesy of National Archives, archives.gov.)

Henrietta Moore Theissen Johnson bears the unsavory distinction of holding the record for most litigious of the cemetery's occupants. She was born to Henry and Cornelia Moore in 1853. Henry later married a woman 34 years his junior, prompting a flurry of legal activity with his daughter as the two battled over money and claims to real estate. Henrietta was generally unsuccessful, despite her persistence. (AFP.)

Henrietta married Jacob Theissen September 30, 1886. Jacob appears to have shared Henrietta's passion for litigation, as he also appeared in legal pleadings both with and without her as a party. He died November 21, 1919, from "carcinoma of tongue," and although his death certificate indicates that he was buried in a cemetery in Bay Village, Ohio, his headstone stands in Lake Shore Cemetery. (ODC.)

Henrietta's second husband was Charles Johnson. Whether by choice or by default, Charles became Henrietta's new partner in litigation. The legal system did not provide well for either of them, as both spent their final days in the county's poorhouse. Henrietta died in 1933, and Charles in 1941. Both are buried in Lake Shore Cemetery, though Charles's grave is unmarked. Buried with Jacob, Henrietta finally holds permanent claim to a piece of Avon Lake property. (ODC.)

Seven
UNDER ONE ROOF BUT DIFFERENT DIRECTIONS

This farmhouse bore witness to the successes and tragedies of generations of the Dunning family and remains standing. Current owners F.J. Tom and Glendalee Burns bought the Avon Lake home in 1973 and worked to maintain as much historical accuracy as possible in its restoration. The house is listed as a historical landmark with the Lorain County Historical Society and the Ohio Historical Society, and its former occupants lived distinctly divergent lives. (Photograph by author.)

If walls could talk and stones could speak, the Dunning home would impart an ample share of this family's stories. Nearly a decade ahead of the potato famine immigrations, Alexander and Margaret Dunning left their home in county Down, Ireland, and traveled with their family to the United States in 1838. They settled in Avon Lake, where they secured 75 acres of land. Son John Dunning later built a home (pictured) at the south end of the property for himself and his family, which was subsequently occupied by his son Charles and the latter's wife and daughters. As may sometimes be the case within families, the Dunning personalities were radically diverse, and the work ethic among the siblings was in sharp contrast. While some were pillars of the community, others conducted themselves in such manner as to besmirch the family name, leaving behind a dismal heritage of embarrassing press and financial indebtedness. (ALPL; Donor: Joseph Cole.)

Somehow persuaded that a better life awaited them in unknown territory, Alexander and Margaret Dunning left Ireland with their six children, sailed to a new continent, and settled upon untamed farmland. Their fearlessness was rewarded, as Alexander was successful in farming and grape-growing along Avon Lake's shore. Joined to a developing community of diverse nationalities, the Dunnings were known among their neighbors as "Orange Irish." Margaret and Alexander are buried with several of their adult children along the easternmost perimeter of Lake Shore Cemetery. Husband and wife lived relatively long lives. Margaret died July 7, 1862, at the age of 74, and her husband died October 18, 1878, at the age of 81. After Margaret's death, Alexander spent his final years at the home of his daughter Elizabeth with her family. Two of Margaret and Alexander's daughters, Catherine and Elizabeth, and two of their sons, Alexander Jr. and John, joined them in the family plot. (AFP.)

Widowed at 29, Catherine Dunning Ketchum had been married not quite 10 years. She was left with four sons, ages nine, six, four, and an infant born shortly after her husband's death from typhoid. When the Civil War began, the two oldest left to join the Union army while just teenagers. Catherine lived to see both sons return, but died a few years later, on October 8, 1868—her eldest son's 24th birthday. (AFP.)

Catherine's third son, Franklyn, was four years old when his father died. By his 12th birthday, his was living on the farm of his paternal aunt and her husband in a neighboring town. Franklyn died on January 2, 1870, less than 15 months after his mother, and is the only one of her sons to be buried with her in Lake Shore Cemetery. His gravestone records his age as "21y 6m." (AFP.)

Catherine is buried near her sister Elizabeth. Just 14 years old when she came from Ireland with her family, Elizabeth married Wolcott Mitchell in 1846. Her obituary of May 1897 describes her as a beloved neighbor, "always first at the bed of sickness." Her husband was the brother of typhoid victim Albert Mitchell, who is buried nearby. Wolcott and Elizabeth had nine children, two of whom are buried with them. Wolcott died April 28, 1905, just three days after a beloved great-grandson. According to his obituary, the family had just returned from the child's funeral when they were called to the man's bedside as he "breathed his last." (AFP.)

Alexander and Margaret Dunning's son John married Mahala Moore, granddaughter of Revolutionary War soldier Joseph Moore, in 1855. John Dunning was a carpenter and farmer, with a substantial farm in Avon Lake. The couple had 11 children, seven of whom survived to adulthood. John died in 1909, and Mahala died in 1923. Five of their children are buried with them, one in an unmarked grave. (AFP.)

John's son Edson (sometimes known as Edward) had a troubled history. In January 1914, he was adjudicated an "incompetent" by Lorain County Probate Court due to chronic alcoholism. A brother, Charles Ernest Dunning, was appointed his guardian. Tragedy ensued in September 1914 when Edson's body—his skull fractured in two places—was found at the foot of a cliff in Avon Lake, generating much speculation and triggering a coroner's inquest. (ODC.)

The inquest, according to a local newspaper, revealed that Dunning and "several associates" had spent the day drinking and gambling. They achieved an "advanced state of intoxication" and parted company. An inebriated Dunning then stumbled off the cliff and fell to his death. His brother, left to untangle the dead man's affairs, purchased a headstone bearing the name Edson Dunning but inscribed with the wrong year of death. (AFP.)

The Dunning family watched history repeat itself over two decades later when Allen Dunning lost his life in a death that uncannily mimicked that of his elder brother Edson. In January 1938, the younger Dunning was reported missing, and a search ensued. Nearly seven days later, the search was called to a halt when his body was found at the bottom of a 45-foot cliff along Lake Erie in Avon Lake behind the home of his employer. Deputies who responded concluded that the 63-year-old man, whose occupation was identified as "gardener," had fallen and landed on the bank below. The cause of his death was listed as "fractured cervical vertebra." Although his death certificate indicates that he was buried in Avon Lake's cemetery, there is no monument remaining to mark his final resting place. (ODC.)

Bertha Dunning Derringer has the distinction of being the longest-lived person to be buried in Lake Shore Cemetery. Born in 1871, she outlived two husbands. She is interred with her second husband, Charles Derringer, with whom she ran a small grocery store. She lived to be 103 years old. (ALPL; Donor: Debra Beard.)

Charles and Bertha Derringer owned Derringer's Grocery Store in Avon Lake, where they both worked. The market's inventory was advertised as "Groceries, Meats, Tobaccos, Candy." Charles died in 1931 at the age of 59, and Bertha continued operating the store for several years before selling it. (AFP.)

The second of the Dunning sons, Charles Ernest Dunning, was a respected pillar of the community. When Avon Lake became a village, he was elected its first treasurer in 1918. He also served as a city assessor and a school board member. Unfortunately, he was burdened with his brother Edson's guardianship. It fell upon Charles to manage Edson's affairs when his brother was committed to St. Joseph's Hospital for treatment. Charles assumed responsibility for payment of the former's debts and care, but when dictated by the need for finances, he filed the necessary probate proceedings to have Edson's share of the family's real estate sold to pay for the hospital confinement. Nine months after taking on guardianship responsibilities, Charles found himself in the sad circumstance of being named executor of his deceased brother's estate. (AFP.)

Dell Bertha Wilcox married Charles Dunning in 1879, leaving behind a career as a school teacher. The community-minded woman later served as a member of Avon Lake's school board. The couple had twin daughters, Nina (pictured) and Nettie. Daughter Nettie, who wrote social columns for a local newspaper, is also buried in Lake Shore Cemetery along with her husband, Fred Engel. (ALPL; Donor: Rosemary Gfell.)

Nina Dunning remained single her entire life. The story that prevails is that she was engaged to be married, but her fiancé died when the ship on which he was a crewman went down in a storm. Nina, bereft at the loss of her betrothed, vowed that she would marry no other. (ALPL; Donor: Rosemary Gfell.)

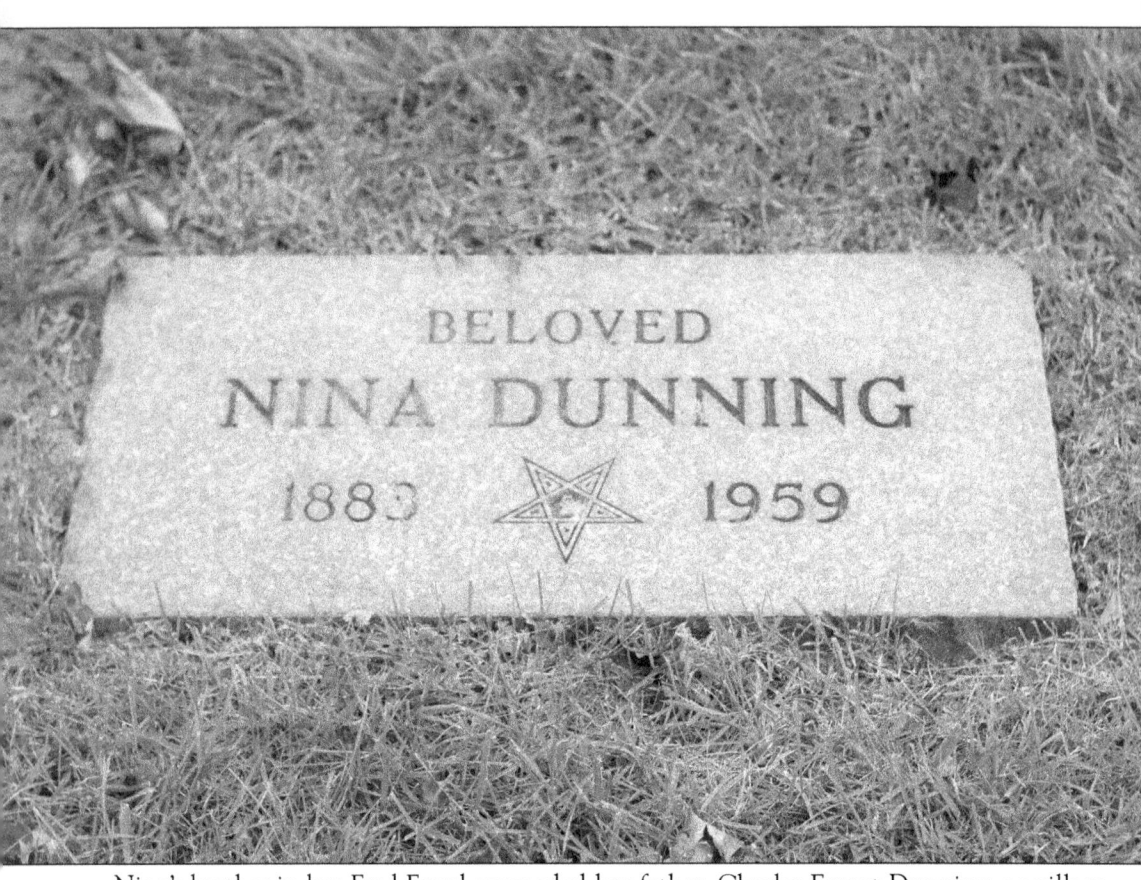

Nina's brother-in-law Fred Engel succeeded her father, Charles Ernest Dunning, as village treasurer. Upon Fred's death, Nina herself carried on the family tradition by being elected treasurer in 1933. She held the position for over 20 years and boasted of never having taken a vacation during her career. She carried out her treasury duties in the family home, which also served as her office, and further served her community as a member of the Poor Relief Committee. City officials could be seen driving to the Dunning house to bring payroll checks for Nina's signature. She remained in the family home until she reached the age of 75 years. Forced to retire when she fell and broke an arm, she died in 1959. She was active in the Eastern Star organization, and members conducted services at her funeral; her headstone bears their insignia. (AFP.)

Eight
TALES FROM BENEATH THE TURF

The burial site of Orlando A. Moore, great-grandson of Revolutionary War veteran Joseph Moore of Lake Shore Cemetery, is memorialized with a Grand Army of the Republic marker. Orlando enlisted in the Union army on February 2, 1863, and served in the Civil War. He was discharged in May 1865. Several years after, he married a young woman in Michigan, but he soon abandoned his bride to sail the lakes. (AFP.)

Orlando Moore later met Eliza Jaycox, daughter of a successful farmer in Avon Lake, and determined to marry her. He consulted a lawyer, whose research suggested that the first wife was deceased. The lawyer advised Orlando that he was free to remarry. A wedding to Miss Jaycox followed in July 1879. (AFP.)

More than 15 years later, Orlando's first wife appeared quite unexpectedly in Avon Lake in search of her errant husband. Humiliated by the scandal, Eliza was described by local newspapers as being "prostrate with grief." A warrant was issued for Orlando's arrest for bigamy, and he fled. He soon reconsidered, returned, and voluntarily surrendered himself. After properly attending to all necessary legal business, a second marriage license was issued for Orlando and Eliza in January 1900. (AFP.)

The intervening years had been especially grievous for Eliza Jaycox Moore. She lost four young children in quick succession between 1882 and 1889; none of them lived much beyond their second birthday. A host of childhood diseases claimed the lives of her offspring, and only her fifth and last child, Leroy, survived to adulthood. While Eliza and Orlando were determined to preserve their marriage, it appears that not all of Eliza's family members were as forgiving. Upon her death in 1911, it was her brother James, and not her husband, who handled final arrangements and purchased the headstone for Eliza that also bears the names of her deceased children. James handled the entire administration of Eliza's estate, which included a receipt to the Electric Package Agency for "transportation of body, consigned to J.M. Jaycox, Stop 49" of Lake Shore Electric Railway. (Author's collection.)

Henry and Caroline Engel stirred speculation and controversy in the community in 1909. They had sold 42 acres of land to a "stranger," whose apparent intent was to build "an aire strip" with "an aeroplane station" upon the Engel farm in Avon Lake. The "aire strip" never materialized, but Caroline again shook the community with her unexpected death in 1910 at the age of 58 when she contracted pneumonia. (AFP.)

Little more than three years after Caroline's death, Henry buried his son George. The 21-year-old electric railway employee had survived typhoid as a child, but he could not overcome the disease that claimed his life on February 17, 1914. The cause of death is listed as "germina of brain," with a secondary cause being attributed to syphilis. Dr. Pipes, also interred in Lake Shore Cemetery, signed the young man's death certificate. (AFP.)

Henry Engle also survived a daughter, Lenora, who drew press attention with her on-again, off-again wedding to Otto Beers. On her wedding day, the groom was a no-show, and waiting guests were sent home. Despite this unpromising beginning, Lenore married Otto after his delayed return, even though he refused explanation for his initial absence. She died in 1920, and Otto remarried shortly thereafter. Lenora's marker is a modest stone near her mother's burial site. (AFP.)

Following Henry's death in 1931, his son Fred died. Fred married Nettie Dunning, and he followed his father-in-law's footsteps as village treasurer. Nettie died in 1926, and although Fred remarried, he remained close with the Dunnings. On May 23, 1933, he died of coronary thrombosis at the Dunning home. He is buried next to Nettie. Oddly, Fred's last name is spelled "Engel" and Nettie's is spelled "Engle" on the couple's adjacent headstones. (AFP.)

William Engel, a railway motorman for 37 years, was the last of Henry's family. He buried his brother Albert in Avon Lake's cemetery in 1942, but the location is unmarked. Married to Mamie Tomanek, William died in 1944. The couple was known for popular social events. William's end came peacefully, at the end of a fishing pier. Daughter Garnet and her husband, Archie Spade, are buried nearby. (AFP.)

Eugene Mitchell, son of Wolcott and Elizabeth Dunning Mitchell, is buried in Lake Shore Cemetery according to his death certificate. Eugene never married. Though generally successful in escaping newspaper notice, he was in the headlines when sued by one Peter Osterman for $15,000 for "alienation of affections." Blaming Mitchell for his failed marriage, Osterman sought compensation. Eugene did ultimately escape public scrutiny after death, as his grave is not marked by a legible headstone. (AFP.)

One colorful local who disrupted community peace was Charles Bilton, who did not find reconciliation with his neighbors until after he was laid to rest with them in Lake Shore Cemetery. Listing his occupation as motorman for the Lake Shore Electric Railway on his marriage application, Bilton had a checkered past. In 1903, he was committed to the Toledo Insane Asylum after terrorizing Norwalk, Ohio, residents when he rode horseback into town, threatening to shoot and kill everyone. In 1909, he married Avon Lake resident Elsie May Hill. Within two years he had antagonized a group of townspeople, who took legal action against him. They availed themselves of relief offered by early Ohio law, pursuant to which probate courts could entertain "Inquest of Lunacy" proceedings. A ruling would result in a finding of insanity, which could be followed by commitment of the "lunatic" to an institution. (AFP.)

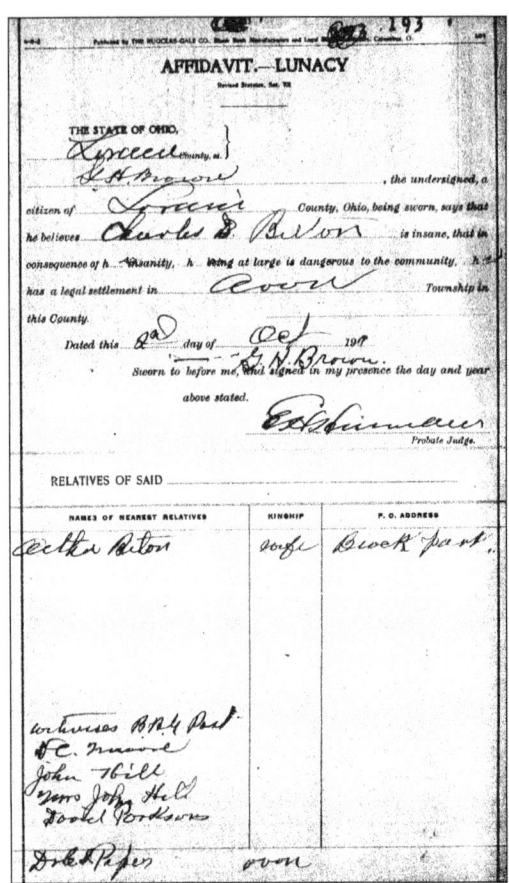

In October 1911, several Avon Lake residents joined in the filing of an affidavit seeking the arrest and commitment of Bilton. The affidavit, pictured here, asks that Bilton be confined in Massillon State Hospital and was filed in Lorain County Probate Court. (Courtesy Judge James Walther, LCPC.)

CHARLES BILTON A HARD ONE TO CATCH

Beach Park Man Fooled Sheriff for Two Days but was Finally Landed

An arrest warrant was issued for Bilton, but his apprehension was not easy. A local newspaper reported that the sheriff was successful only by "swooping down" on Bilton in the night, the latter having loaded all his household goods on a wagon in anticipation of leaving town quickly. The sheriff's efforts were for naught. At the hearing that followed, Bilton was found "not insane" by the probate judge. (LCPC.)

Bilton's wife, Elsie, died April 14, 1919, while she and Charles were living in Chicago. She left behind two young daughters—eight-year-old Florence and six-year-old Dorothy. The care of the girls was assumed by Elsie's mother, Ida French Hill. Ida was living in Avon Lake, where Elsie's body was brought for burial. Elsie was joined by her sister Edna Sanders, who died April 14, 1919, and was also buried in Lake Shore Cemetery. (AFP.)

Florence Bilton died May 19, 1968, in Washington, DC, just two months after the death of her father, Charles. Florence was 56 at the time of her death, was unmarried, and left no heirs. She is buried near her father's grave. The burial sites of her grandparents John and Ida French Hill are a short distance from her final place of repose. (AFP.)

The burial sites of John T. and Ida French Hill, Edna and Elsie's parents, are marked by a solid monument. It is inscribed with the couple's names, and the names of their two daughters and two sons. There are no death dates for their sons, and no record that the men are buried there. The Hills' proximity to Charles Bilton's grave is ironic, as their signatures appear among those on the lunacy affidavit that had been filed against Bilton. (AFP.)

Charlotte "Lottie" Goepp, eldest daughter of German immigrant Jacob Goepp, worked "dressing feathers" as a young adult. After an unsuccessful first marriage, she married Cleveland businessman Charles App. Charles disappeared on June 2, 1921, and a search was undertaken by police and a local sheriff's department. Speculation was rampant that foul play was involved and that App had been robbed of a large sum of money in his possession, then murdered. (AFP.)

The 63-year-old manager of the Cleveland Audit Company was found a day later, lying in a field near his summer home in Avon Lake. Discoloration of his body was thought to be bruising sustained as the result of an assault. An autopsy was performed, which discredited the murder theory, as cause of death was determined to be "apoplexy"—a heart attack. (ODC.)

App was found with a watch and chain and $19.53 on his person, but the family persisted in their contention that a theft had been perpetrated. They maintained that the deceased had left his home with significantly more cash in his possession. Robbery was not borne out by any evidence. Lottie buried her husband in Lake Shore Cemetery, and then joined him there in 1953. (AFP.)

Lottie and her younger sister Harriette Goepp Grosse both died in 1953. Harriette is the only Goepp family member not buried in Lake Shore Cemetery. Sister Phoena Goepp Smith, a 35-year resident of Avon Lake, lived to celebrate her 99th birthday and was interred with the Goepp family in 1961. (AFP.)

The youngest daughter, Olive, married Clevelander John Dolman in September 1900. He was 32, and she was 20. He listed his occupation as architect, and she showed none. The couple had one child, Hazel, in 1901. John died in May 1925 and is buried in Cleveland. Olive was left with substantial assets, including a rental cottage, which she leased to tourists. (ALPL; Donor – Barney Klement.)

Olive did not lead a quiet life in Avon Lake. In 1943, she was charged with assault and battery, for which she was found guilty in mayor's court and assessed a fine and costs. Upon her refusal to pay, she was jailed for three days. She countered with a $50,000 lawsuit against the mayor, claiming that he lacked jurisdiction in the matter. Her action was dismissed in 1944. (AFP.)

A little more than a year after John Dolman's death, his daughter Hazel Dolman's engagement to Alfred Winter was announced. Hazel was buried in Lake Shore Cemetery in 1990. Alfred and Hazel's daughter Charlotte Winter, who served as Avon Lake Municipal Court clerk until her retirement, was buried with her mother in 1999. Charlotte's death date is missing from her stone. (AFP.)

Daniel Green married Caroline Deeg on June 14, 1849. His bride and her family had endured a 33-day voyage from Germany in 1842, then made their way to Avon Lake where they settled. Caroline was 18 years old when she and Daniel married, and by 1880, husband and wife owned a farm of over 55 acres. The couple raised 10 children, including three sons who brought a great measure of disgrace into the lives of their parents. (AFP.)

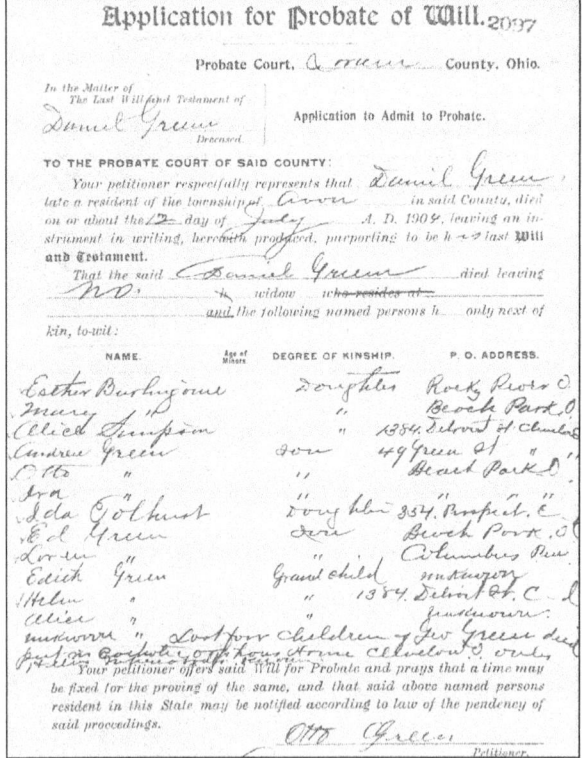

The couple's sons served multiple periods of incarceration for various crimes committed against their neighbors. In December 1903, Caroline died of pneumonia. In May 1904, a guardian was appointed for the widower, Daniel, who had "lost his mind" over his wayward sons, according to a local newspaper report. The guardianship was of short duration, as the disconsolate man died July 12, 1904. His estate was depleted by debt, leaving nothing for his survivors. (LCPC.)

Daughter Ida Green married Henry Knechtges, who was laid to rest in Lake Shore Cemetery in 1897 after unsuccessful treatment at the Newburg asylum, where he was sent for "softening of the brain," according to local news reports. He was remembered as a sober, industrious man, "devotedly attached to his wife and baby daughter." Ida remarried, but she was buried with Henry upon her death in 1842. She has no marker. (AFP.)

Caroline Knechtges, daughter of Ida and Henry, married John Pachis, a native of Greece who immigrated in 1905 and became a naturalized citizen. He served in the military, and died in 1967. Caroline died in 1970 and is buried with her family. No headstone is found for her, but an unmarked open space adjoins her husband's plot. (AFP.)

Alice Simpson, daughter of Daniel and Caroline Green, and her husband, Charles, are both interred in the family plot. Married by the time she was 17 to 40-year-old Charles, Alice was a dressmaker, and her husband was a painter and decorator. The couple had no biological children, and Alice was widowed in 1911 when she was 40. (AFP.)

Charles's demise came when he was knocked over by a horse while crossing a street in front of an oncoming wagon. The horse's hoof struck his head and fractured his skull. He lingered for 24 hours and left his widow with an insolvent estate. She nevertheless secured a beautiful monument for her husband with his birth and death dates. Her name joins his, but her death date of 1929 was never inscribed. (Courtesy of Cuyahoga County Probate Court.)

Selden Payne enlisted in the Union army at the age of 22 during the Civil War. Upon completion of his service, he mustered out in 1865 at Johnson's Island, Sandusky, Ohio. Payne returned to Avon Lake, where he engaged in farming and raised a family with his wife, Laura. In 1891, in declining health, he filed an application for an Army pension as an invalid. (AFP.)

Payne died in 1898 when he unintentionally stepped into the path of an oncoming Lake Shore Electric Railway car. Having suffered much hearing loss, the man neither heard nor saw the oncoming car and was killed instantly. Newspapers reported that Payne, barely 60 years old, was the Lake Shore Electric Railway's first casualty. (Courtesy of Thomas Patton.)

Laura Mitchell Payne, Selden's widow, brought a lawsuit against the railway company after her husband's death. The litigation languished for two years. Finally, in 1900, she received a total of $95 for her loss, and each of her five children received one dollar. Her signature on the settlement document is a simple X. (LCPC.)

Near tragedy struck a second time when Laura almost suffered a fate similar to that of her husband. In April 1900, she was hit by a Lake Shore Electric Railway car while attempting to cross the track en route to visit her daughter. She was thrown several feet and sustained injuries to her arm and ribs, but survived. (AFP.)

Several of Selden and Laura's family are buried nearby. Daughter Ada and her husband are both interred in Lake Shore Cemetery. Despite the family's unfortunate history with the Lake Shore Electric Railway, Ada married Albert "Bert" Conklin, a railway motorman. Though the pair lived relatively long lives, they lost one of their two sons when the boy was quite young. (AFP.)

The Conklins' five-year-old child, Leonard, is interred in a nearby plot. A victim of drowning in Lake Erie, the youth died on April 25, 1905. The local newspaper reported that a "sad feature" connected with the boy's death was the demise of his elderly grandfather, Walcott Mitchell, who survived the tragic news but a few days. (AFP.)

Carl, who was also a motorman for the Lake Shore Electric Railway, was the last of Selden and Laura's offspring to be buried in Lake Shore Cemetery. He shares a headstone with his wife, Lora, who died in 1950. Although Carl's stone bears no death date, he died in 1963. (AFP.)

Carl and Lora are buried next to their son-in-law George Vaughn. On December 18, 1937, at the age of 32, Vaughn was involved in an automobile collision. Emergency surgery was unsuccessful, and he succumbed the following day. His death certificate attributes his demise to "extensive 1st and 2nd degree burns of body." The auto was destroyed by fire, with Vaughn its helpless victim. (AFP.)

The Mawby family occupies four burial plots. Mathias Mawby Sr., born in 1847 in England, was a fruit farmer. In 1919, he became another of the railway's victims. When he was struck by a railcar while crossing the tracks that traversed his farm, his arm, leg, and 13 ribs were broken and his spinal cord damaged. Mawby filed a lawsuit, claiming the approaching railway car had given no warning. He survived, but with permanent injuries. He died in 1932. (AFP.)

Mathias Sr. and Mary Ann Brichford were married in 1883, and had three children. Their second child, John, born in 1886, lived only 17 days and is buried in neighboring Bay Village's Lakeside Cemetery. Mary Ann died of stomach cancer in 1924 at the age of 67. Her husband, despite his multiple injuries received from the railway car, survived her by eight years. (AFP.)

The Mawbys' daughter Lucy was born in 1884. She never married and occupied the family home after her parents' death until the time of her own demise. She was an independent and self-sufficient woman, who generated income by renting rooms to tourists in Avon Lake near its attractive Lake Erie shore. A charter member of the Avon Lake Congregational Church, Lucy also served as organist there for many years. (ALPL; Donor: Barney Klement.)

Lucy died in 1965. She was survived by her brother Mathias Jr., who made his living as a carpenter. Mathias Jr. died at the home of his daughter in Edmonds, Washington, in 1974, and his body was brought back to Avon Lake for burial with Lucy and their parents. (AFP.)

Buried with the Mawbys is Henry Walker, grandson of John Walker Sr., for whom Walker Road—which spans the width of the city—was named. The only Walker buried in Avon Lake, Henry led a life of little note. His paternal grandmother was a Mawby, and those were the family members with whom he most closely aligned. Before his own death, he provided grave-digging services for at least two other burials located near his own final resting place. (AFP.)

Dr. John Pipes signed the death certificates of many whom he later joined in Lake Shore Cemetery. He was twice elected mayor in Avon before relocating to Avon Lake in 1921, and was there elected mayor in 1926, serving two more terms. As community physician, he even rendered veterinary care when necessary. When weather made roads impassable, he rode on horseback to tend the sick. His home is pictured here. (ALPL; Donor: Gerry Paine.)

Pipes once served as president of the Lorain County Medical Association and was a founder and first president of a telephone company that provided service in the areas of which he was later elected mayor. While serving in office in Avon Lake, Pipes devoted substantial time in mayor's court to hearing and pronouncing sentence in Prohibition violation cases. (AFP.)

Dr. Pipes died in 1932 and was survived by his wife, Caroline, by 22 years. A graduate of the Cleveland Art School, she married John at the famed Hollenden Hotel in Cleveland in 1901. Involved in both city government and public health matters, she served as village treasurer and on the library board. During World War I, she received a citation for her work with the Red Cross. (AFP.)

The predominantly rural Avon Lake community was, like much of America in the 1920s, distressed by the nation's shift to industrialism. As this move generated a resurgence of the Ku Klux Klan and prompted a US House of Representatives committee investigation in 1921 (pictured), the movement infiltrated even Avon Lake, generating fear and disquietude within the community. Lake Shore Cemetery holds the remains of one of the organization's local leaders, Arthur Buswell. A farmer, Buswell drew a crowd during his Easter Sunday funeral procession in 1924 when his remains were ceremoniously escorted to Lake Shore Cemetery by 1,200 white-robed Klansmen. One newspaper carried a front-page photograph of the hooded men, shoulder to shoulder, tightly encircling the cemetery's perimeter. His wife, Elizabeth, survived him by 18 years and is buried with him. (Creator unknown. House Committee Investigating the Ku Klux Klan. 1921. Photograph. Library of Congress Prints and Photographs Online Catalog, www.loc.gov/item/94506040.)

Described by the press as a man "widely known throughout the communities," Buswell enjoyed prominence in an organization that eschewed bootleggers, but he was posthumously snubbed by his brother Charles. The latter was arrested in 1928 for hosting a raucous alcohol house party that generated complaints from neighbors. That, too, made the press. (AFP.)

Nine
LIVES WELL LIVED

The arrest that interrupted Charles Buswell's illicit party was conducted by two deputies. One of those was Henry Brodie, an early law enforcement agent in the village. Active during Prohibition and successful in the confiscation of smuggled alcohol and the arrest of violators, he bore the nickname "Two-Gun Brodie." (ALPL; Donor: Ronald Thomas.)

Henry and his wife, Lillian Rees Brodie, operated a restaurant across from the illuminating plant on the shore. While the building was being erected, they served the construction workers, and upon completion, their trade was sustained by plant employees. Two nieces who came to live with the Brodies upon their mother's death helped in the family's restaurant. Henry was later employed by the Cleveland Electric Illuminating Company. (Courtesy of Cleveland Press; Cleveland Memory Project.)

Henry's death certificate lists his occupation as watchman at the "power house." The relationship between Brodie and that company was at times acrimonious, even leading to litigation when Brodie accused the latter of encroaching upon his property, which adjoined the plant's property. Although the affected property was not substantial, Brodie held his ground in fending off the encroacher. (AFP.)

Lillian Brodie is credited with having made a five-foot-by-eight-foot flag bearing 37 stars representing Avon Lake men who served in World War I. Created in celebration of the safe return of their own son, Dudley (front row, fifth from left), the flag was presented September 6, 1919, at a dinner-dance hosted for the returned soldiers. (ALPL; Donor: John Earley.)

It was Lillian's original intent that the flag hang in Avon Lake High School (pictured), from which her son had graduated. After the flag was displayed there for many years, renovations were made to the school, and the flag was removed. It had been kept in storage for an extended period, but it was eventually restored and framed and is now on display in the Avon Lake Public Library. (ALPL; Donor: Nancy Abram.)

Committed to the care of their extended family, Lillian and Henry raised two nieces and a nephew when the children's mother died. Another niece, Elora, is buried not far from Lillian's grave. While Lillian endured her son's absence and celebrated his return from World War I, Elora's story of grief and triumph over loss as she endured tragedy during World War II is even more compelling. (AFP.)

Elora Rees married Clifford Hamilton (front row, second from right), gunner/armorer on a B-24 Liberator fighting Japanese forces in World War II. Crewmate and best friend Pasquale Gerrone (front row, second from left) was grounded for illness from a mission over the South China Sea on May 20, 1944, when the plane was shot down and the entire crew lost. Elora was left a widow with an infant daughter. (Courtesy of Braydon L. Hassinger via Jana Churchwell Scott, findagrave.com.)

A turret gunner/waist gunner, Gerrone joined another crew, earning the Distinguished Flying Cross, two air medals, and multiple other honors. Forced to parachute from his plane in another mission, he survived, but wandered lost for days before being aided by American missionaries. He was honorably discharged in September 1945 and resolved to honor Hamilton's memory by assuring the well-being of his widow. (Courtesy of National Archives, archives.gov.)

Gerrone's concern was favorably received, and a courtship ensued. Following an official proclamation of Hamilton's death by the Army (listed on their marriage application as February 21, 1946), Pasquale "Patsy" Gerrone and Elora Rees Hamilton were married on June 22, 1946. The occasion was a joyous one, with the bride attired in a white wedding gown and attended by six bridesmaids and two flower girls. (Pennsylvania Marriages, 1852–1968, FamilySearch.org.)

The couple was married 67 years. Patsy raised Clifford's daughter as his own, and the couple had four more sons together. He was employed by the Avon Lake Board of Education as chief of buildings and grounds, and served as a volunteer fireman for 25 years with the Avon Lake Fire Department. Patsy died in October 2013 at the age of 91, and Elora died four years later in October 2017, at the same age. (AFP.)

Ten

TENDING THE CEMETERY

As would be expected with an old cemetery, many remnants of monuments exist that no longer identify the occupant beneath. Some grassy plots have rectangular traces but no markers. Such is the case with Douglas Bouse, a two-year-old with no headstone. Son of Hugo Bouse, one of Avon Lake's first mayors, the child was scalded to death when he fell into a bathtub filled with hot water. (ODC.)

Numerous death certificates reveal the names of persons like little Douglas who are interred in Lake Shore Cemetery but whose specific burial sites cannot be determined. Unmarked plots within the graveyard appear to be unclaimed but beg not to be disturbed. The first to put any semblance of order to burials and interment locations in Lake Shore Cemetery was Fred Burmeister. (ALPL; Donor: William Burmeister.)

Fred Burmeister was founder of the city's first and only funeral home, and it was he who began maintaining records of burials in the 1940s. Prior to his efforts, unmarked graves were sometimes inadvertently disturbed when ground was opened for interment, necessitating that the grave be relocated and dug anew. (ALPL; Donor: William Burmeister.)

Numerous burials in Lake Shore Cemetery were overseen by the city's pioneer funeral director. The original funeral home was expanded, and the Burmeister family lived on the second floor of the home, which was located near the center of town. The thriving operation was furthered by successive generations of Burmeisters who have continued to develop and enhance the business. (ALPL; Donor: William Burmeister.)

Throughout its existence, Avon Lake's cemetery has gone through intermittent periods of neglect and dilapidation. In 1897, a committee of 17 interested citizens joined together for the purpose of restoring and improving the city's only burial ground. With their teams of horses, they brought several loads of dirt to grade the grounds and construct walks. Matthias Mawby Sr. was appointed cemetery sexton, and was later interred in the very ground he once kept. (AFP.)

The maintenance needs of the cemetery outlasted those early custodians, and the site again fell into disrepair. In 2004, Veterans of Foreign Wars Post 8796 of Avon Lake committed itself to restoring the cemetery. Co-founded by World War II veteran John Robertson in 1964, the organization achieved successful results. What could easily have become an overlooked and forgotten burial site became instead a community restoration project. (AFP.)

The stone interment shelter was renovated when the Veterans of Foreign Wars, the Kiwanis, and Avon Lake's PolyOne Corporation joined forces and made needed improvements. A memorial stone was installed, pavers were laid, the VFW post purchased flags, and the city installed flagpoles. In 2004, Avon Lake's citizens, businesses, and civic groups were given the opportunity to purchase pavers engraved with the names and service information of servicemen and women of their choosing. (Courtesy of Tony Tomanek.)

The cemetery was designated a landmark by the Lorain County Historical Society in October 2005, and a marker was placed commemorating the event. In May 2009, John Shondel of American Legion Post 211 procured new headstones for three of the cemetery's Civil War veterans, and an unveiling was held in May 2010. In May 2013, the cemetery received an additional designation as a historic landmark from the Avon Lake Historic Preservation Commission. (Courtesy of Tony Tomanek.)

Continuing the long-standing tradition of a solemn Memorial Day march to Lake Shore Cemetery to remember its fallen heroes, the City of Avon Lake assumed the coordinating responsibilities for the celebration in 2018. In this most fitting place to pay tribute, the event is an impressive visual reminder of the sacrifices made by many. (Courtesy of Tony Tomanek.)

In a moving Memorial Day ceremony conducted at the cemetery each year, the roll of names of locals who have served in various wars is read. A moment of silence follows in memory and recognition of those who have gone on. The Revolutionary War, the War of 1812, the Civil War, World War I, and World War II are all represented in the annual roll call of veterans. (Courtesy of Tony Tomanek.)

Now maintained by the city, the historic burial ground draws visitors both young and old, the curious, and those who seek to know the city's past. Here, the great-great-great-granddaughter of Anton Tomanek walks barefoot over the grounds that hold a multitude of her ancestors. (Courtesy of Tony Tomanek.)

Not only are all available burial sites in Lake Shore Cemetery claimed, but there is no expectation of growth. To the immediate west is a private residence, the border between house and graveyard delineated by no more than a wood fence that closely abuts several of the graves. (AFP.)

Originally owned by Thomas and Georgia Wood, the stone house that competes with the cemetery for space has long generated interest. Lorain County auditor's records indicate a construction date around 1880, but the actual completion date is unknown. One historian recounts that the home was built with stones unearthed in the fields of local farmers, who were happy to be rid of them. Once their purpose was discovered, the farmers began charging for the stones. (AFP.)

Behind the house, flanking the lakeshore and keeping silent watch over the burial ground, is a distinctive and iconic structure that identifies the location of the otherwise obscure cemetery. It commands notice by any who pass by. Originally an icehouse, it has four stories with nearly four-foot-thick walls. Ice was once cut from Lake Erie during the winter months and packed in straw or sawdust, layered, and stored to be used as refrigeration for perishable foods during the summer months. For those of means, ice was also used to chill summer beverages. As ice pieces were cut from the frozen lake, they were pulled up to the icehouse by a horse-drawn winch. Ice harvesting was essential until the mid-1940s when refrigerators began to secure their place in residential homes. That the icehouse remains standing is not surprising. The more interesting feature is that the cemetery's interment shelter and the icehouse are so perfectly matched. (AFP.)

Through the efforts of many, restoration of Lake Shore Cemetery has been successful, and it continues to provide a link to the community's past. While few vestiges of history remain intact from the city's earliest beginnings, Avon Lake's deepest history lies beneath its ground along Lake Erie's shore. It is hoped that this book will preserve the stories of those who rest beneath. (Courtesy of Tony Tomanek.)

Visit us at
arcadiapublishing.com

www.ingramcontent.com/pod-product-compliance
Lightning Source LLC
Chambersburg PA
CBHW060937170426
43194CB00027B/2984